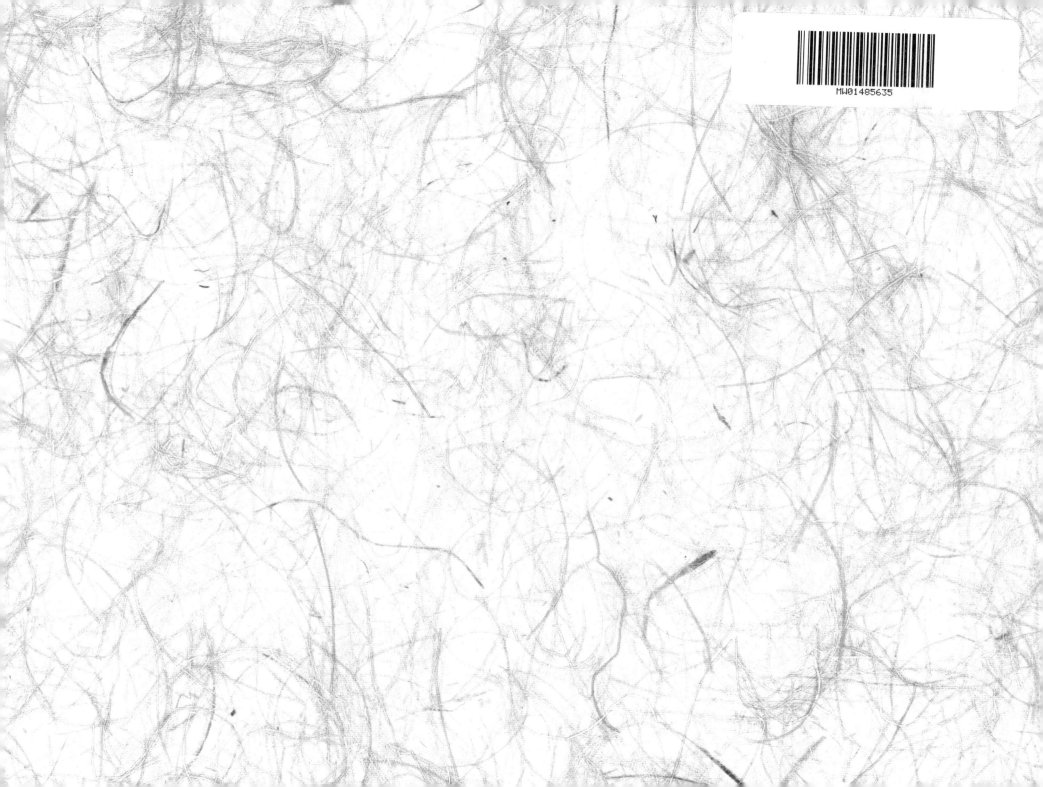

Contemporary Hopi Kachina Dolls

Nancy N. Schiffer

Schiffer Publishing Ltd®

4880 Lower Valley Road, Atglen, PA 19310 USA

Acknowledgments

I am indebted to many people for their help toward the production of this book. At Beyond Native Tradition Gallery, Holbrook, Arizona: Beverly McGee. At McGee's Arts & Crafts, Keams Canyon, Arizona: Bruce McGee, Verlinda, Brandon Bosworth, and Elene Atokuku. At Palms Trading Co, Albuquerque, New Mexico: Guy Berger, Diana Berger, Lyle Pino, and Victoria Archuleta. Bruce M. Waters for all the photography and his good nature on our trips to the collections, and those who prefer to remain anonymous. Thank you all.

Title Page: **Eagle** kachina, *Kwahu*, dancing out of a pottery bowl, by Lomahquahtu, 22" h.

Library of Congress Cataloging-in-Publication Data

Schiffer, Nancy.
  Contemporary hopi kachina dolls / by Nancy N. Schiffer.
    p. cm.
  ISBN 0-7643-1848-9 (Hardcover)
  1. Kachina dolls--Themes, motives. 2. Hopi dolls--Themes, motives.
  I. Title.
  E99.H7S324 2003
  745.592'21'089974--dc21

                        2003001554

Designed by Mark David Bowyer
Type set in Impact/Humanist521 BT

ISBN: 0-7643-1848-9
Printed in China

Published by Schiffer Publishing Ltd.
4880 Lower Valley Road
Atglen, PA 19310
Phone: (610) 593-1777; Fax: (610) 593-2002
E-mail: Schifferbk@aol.com
Please visit our web site catalog at **www.schifferbooks.com**
We are always looking for people to write books on new and related subjects. If you have an idea for a book, please contact us at the above address.

This book may be purchased from the publisher.
Include $3.95 for shipping. Please try your bookstore first.
You may write for a free catalog.

In Europe, Schiffer books are distributed by
Bushwood Books
6 Marksbury Ave. Kew Gardens
Surrey TW9 4JF England
Phone: 44 (0)20 8392-8585; Fax: 44 (0)20 8392-9876
E-mail: Bushwd@aol.com
Free postage in the UK. Europe: air mail at cost.
Please try your bookstore first.

Contents

Introduction

The cycle of Hopi kachina dance ceremonies extends from December 21, the winter solstice, until after June 21, the summer solstice, according to the following schedule:

Winter Solstice, *Soyala*
December 21
Kiva Dances, *Pamuya*
January
Bean Dance, *Powamu*
February

Repeat Dances, *Anktioni*
March
Plaza Dances, *Soyohim*
April
Plaza Dances, *Soyohim*
May
Summer Solstice
June 21
Home Dance, *Niman*
July

After Niman, the kachinas have departed for their spiritual home and the Hopi ceremonies are conducted without them. Women and men participate in their respective roles according to the following schedule.

Snake or Flute Ceremony
August
Women's Society Ceremony, *Marau*
September
Women's Society Ceremony, *Oaqole*
October
Tribal Initiation Ceremony, *Wuwuchim*
November

With new initiates in place, the cycle once more begins in December with the newly trained kachina dancers for the winter solstice, *Soyala*.

Colors

Paint colors often indicate one of six directions to the Hopi kachina carver:
Yellow- North
Blue or Green- West
Red- South
White- East
Black- Above, zenith
Grey or multicolored- Below, nadir

Three flat kachina **Crib Toys**, *Tihu*, 6" h.

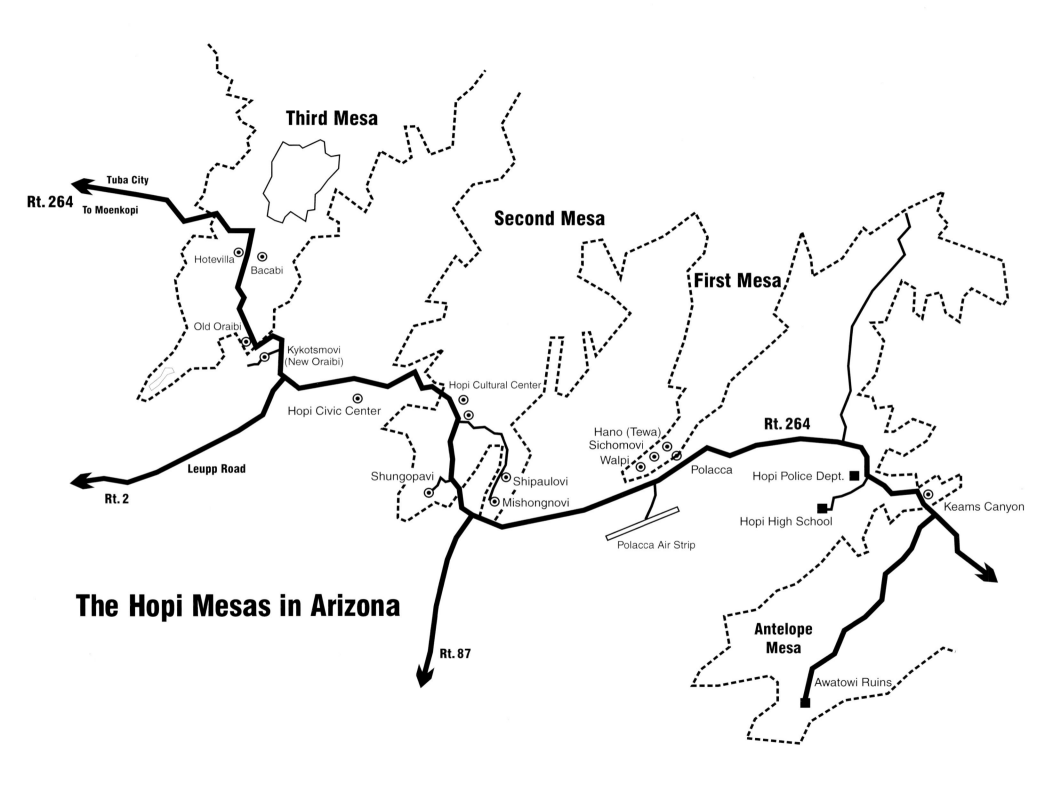

The Hopi Mesas in Arizona

Crow Mother kachina, *Angwushnasomitaka* by G. Hayah, 10" h. and **Double-face Butterfly Maiden** kachina, *Poli Mana*, by G. Hayah, 9-1/2" h.

Miniature **Mudhead Clown**, *Koyemsi*, by E. Felter Jr. of Hotevilla, 3" h. and the legendary non-kachina **Warrior Mouse**, by Loren David, 5-1/2" h.

Weather and Natural Forces

Sun kachina, *Tawa kachina*, by Keith Torres, 11-1/2" h. The Tawa deity interacts with people, animals, and monsters. The kachina dances in the Mixed Dance as a regular participant and not in any major ceremonial events.

Sun kachina, *Tawa kachina*, by Ron Duwyenie, 8" h.

10

Sun kachina, *Tawa kachina*, by Brendan Kayquoptewa, 14-1/2" h.

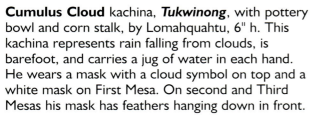

Cumulus Cloud kachina, *Tukwinong*, with pottery bowl and corn stalk, by Lomahquahtu, 6" h. This kachina represents rain falling from clouds, is barefoot, and carries a jug of water in each hand. He wears a mask with a cloud symbol on top and a white mask on First Mesa. On second and Third Mesas his mask has feathers hanging down in front.

Early Morning Singer kachina, *Talavai*, carrying a pine tree, by Brendan Kayquoptewa, 10" h. Originally, Talavai woke Hopi villagers by singing in the early morning and ringing their bells. They appear in the Bean Dance, Powamu Ceremony, standing next to the procession.

Early Morning Singer kachina, *Talavai,* with pine tree, by *Kocha Hon Mana,* Jocelyn Honani-Vote, Hopi, 11-1/2" h.

Early Morning Singer kachina, *Talavai*, by L. Honyuti, 14-3/4" h.

13

Early Morning Singer kachina, *Talavai*, with pine tree, by Brian Kayqueptewa, 10-1/4" h.

Early Morning Singer kachina, *Talavai*, 9" h., mounted on a flat board painted with an eagle, by Rod Philips, 22" h.

Left and above:
Early Morning Singer kachina, *Talavai*, byVernon Laban, 13-1/2" h.

Shooting Thunder kachina, *Umtoinaqa*, by Leo Lacapa, 13-1/2" h. Umtoinaqa is a guard at the Bean Dance, Powamu Ceremony, in February and in Mixed Kachina Dances. He carries the bull roarer in his right hand to imitate the sound of thunder and a bow in his left hand.

Lightning kachina, *Talawipiki*, by Willman Hyeoma, 8-1/4" h.

Kachina set **Lightning Boy** and **Kachina Mother** or **Pour Water Woman**, *Hahai-i Wuhti*, by Wilfred Kaye, 12-1/2" h.

Fire God kachina, *Sulawitsie,* painting a cradle doll, by Sheldon Talas, Polacca, 6" h.

Ashes kachina, *Qootsvu* or *Qochaf,*. 12" h. It is the role of this kachina to purify everything and everyone before the *Pamuya* Ceremony begins in January. It is not often carved

Death kachina, *Masaúu,* by Cecil Kalnimptewa, 15" h.

Death or **Skeleton** kachina, *Masaúu*, by L. Honyouti, 11-1/2" h. This is the only kachina that does not go home at the Niman Ceremony, so he can dance throughout the year. His actions are in opposites, because death is the opposite of life.

Death kachina, *Masaúu,* by Horace Kayqueptewa, 8-3/4" h.

19

Flute kachina, *Lenang*, by Larry David, Tewa, 9" h.

Rattle with black fur headpiece, by Fred Chapella, 10-1/2" h.

Rattle painted green, representing one of the **Twin War Gods**, by Pat Howesa, 12" h.

21

Spirits

Chief kachina, *Eototo*, by Henry Naha 10" h. Eototo knows all the ceremonies and is called the father of the kachinas. He controls the seasons. During the Bean Dance, Powamu Ceremony, on Third Mesa, he draws cloud symbols in corn flour on the ground pointing into the village to draw the clouds and nurturing moisture into the village.

Chief kachina, *Eotote*, by Tino Youvella, Hopi-Tewa, 9" h.

Chief kachina, *Eototo*, by Preston Ami, Tewa Hopi, 10" h.

Kokoshoya, by P. Sewemaenewa, Hopi, 12-1/2" h. He appears as a young boy on Second Mesa with the Chief Kachinas Aholi and Eototo, during the Bean Dance, Powamu Ceremony, in February. As the **Barter** kachina, *Kokosori*, he is borrowed from the Zuni **Fire God,** or *Shlawitsi*. He appears as a young boy at First Mesa in the Pamuya ceremony in January.

Chief's Lieutenant kachina, *Aholi*, by Henry Naha, 3" h. He appears only on Third Mesa during the Bean Dance, Powamu Ceremony, in February. When the Chief, Eototo, makes a cloud mark on the ground, Aholi places his staff on the mark and shouts "Aholi," as though he is reinforcing Eototo's action.

Chief, *Eototo,* and **Lieutenant**, ***Aholi,*** set of kachinas, by Sheldon Talas, 7" h.

Chief, *Eototo,* **and Lieutenant,** *Aholi,* set of kachinas, by Roger Suetopka, 12-3/4" h.

Lieutenant kachina, *Aholi*, by Tino Youvella, Hopi Tewa, 14" h.

Lieutenant kachina, *Aholi*, by Tino Youvella, Hopi Tewa, 11" h.

29

Blue Guard kachina, *Sakw-ahote*, by A. Homoni, 18" h. The guard, or hunter kachina, *Ahote*, shows directions with his coloring: North, yellow; West, blue or green; South, red; and East, white. He performs in the Plaza Dances, in April, and Mixed Kachina Dances. He usually is shown with a hunting bow and rattle or yucca stem.

Blue Guard kachina, *Sakw-ahote,* with long feather bonnet, by H. Naha, 13-1/2" h.

Blue Guard kachina, *Sakw-ahote*, by Leo Lacapa, 12" h.

31

Blue Guard kachina, *Sakw-ahote*, by *Kocha Hon Mana*, Hopi, 17" h.

Blue Guard kachina, *Sakw-ahote*, by Alicia M. Youvella, First Mesa, 13" h.

Yellow Guard kachina, *Siky-ahote*, by Leo
Lacapa, Hopi, 12-1/4" h.

Yellow Guard kachina, *Siky-ahote*, by Tsinnie, 16-1/2" h.

33

Broadface kachina, *Wuyak-kuita*, by Malcolm Fred, 15-5/8" h. This guard kachina prevents problems on the pathway of the advancing kachinas. He terrifies the mischievous clowns as he enforces good behavior.

Warrior kachina, *Chakwaina*, by Tino Youvella, First Mesa, 12" h. This is a mighty warrior whose history goes back to pueblo peoples from the east in former times. His ancestral spirit is highly respected.

Ogre kachina, **Chaveyo**, by Preston Ami, 12" h. Husband of *Hahai-I Wuhti* and father of the *Nataskas*, this kachina scolds the people who shirk their responsibilities to the community. He appears at the spring dances, especially the Water Serpent Dance. He is a giant, and usually depicted in an angry attitude.

Zuni Ogre Scavinger kachina, **Alocle**, by Tino Youvella, First Mesa, 13-3/4" h.

35

Comanchi kachina, *Tutumsi*, by Tino Youvella, 10-1/2" h.
This is a rare kachina who appears at the Mixed Dance.

Crazy Rattle, **Runner**, or **Guard** kachina, *Tuskiapaya*, by
L. Hanyouti, 12-1/2" h. This rattle kachina has black blocks
across his head. He dances at Plaza Dances in the Spring.

Farmer kachina, *Heheya*, by Wayne Poleahla, 16" h. This kachina is a line dancer at the ceremonies.

Farmer kachina, *Heheya*, by Brian Honyouti, 11-1/2" h.

Chief and Germ God kachina, *Ahola*, with yellow and green mask, 15-1/2" h.

38

Chief and **Germ God** kachina, *Ahola*, by Jefferson James Nuvahongnaya, 14" h. *Ahola* is responsible for reproduction and germination in all things who opens the Bean Dance, *Powamu* Ceremony, in February, on First Mesa and Second Mesa. He is the ancient one of the Kachina Clan who led the people to their present homes on the mesas. He distributes bean and corn plants and asks the sun for good crops.

Chief and **Germ God** kachina, *Ahola*, by H. Naha, 12" h.

Chief and **Germ God** kachina, *Ahola*, by Henry Naha, 14-3/4" h.

Chief and **Germ God** kachina, *Ahola*, by Preston Youvella, 9-1/4" h.

Home Dance kachina, ***Hemis***, in a dancing position with an elaborate tablita and carrying a rattle, by Malcolm Fred, 18" h.

Hemis Kachina is the only kachina in the *Niman* Ceremony in July, bringing entire corn plants, the first harvest, to the people. Since their jobs of bringing rain and crops are now finished, the Kachinas return to their homes in the mountains. Niman is the final ceremony of the kachinas, so it is reverent and dignified.

Left-handed Hunter kachina, *Suy-ang-e vif*, with a rabbit, by Henry Naha, 7-1/2" h. The quiver for this kachina is reversed, so that he must use his right hand to draw his arrows. He is a hunting kachina and usually has half his body painted in stripes. He often carries small game

Left-handed Hunter kachina, *Suy-ang-e vif*, by Ronald Adams, 7-1/4" h.

Left Handed Hunter kachina, *Suy-ang-e vif*, by
Fred Chapella, 6" h.

Left Handed Hunter kachina, *Suy-ang-e vif*,
in black mask, by *Kocha Hon Mana*, Jocelyn
Honani-Vote, Hopi, 13" h.

Left-handed Hunter
kachina, *Suy-ang-e vif*, by
H. M. Polequaptewa,
12-1/2" h.

Left-handed Hunter kachina, *Suy-ang-e vif*, by L.Grover, Jr. 10-1/2" h.

Longhair kachina, ***Angak'china***, in a dancing position, by Duane Hyeoma, 11" h. Longhair kachinas appear in a group, often singing, to bring rain. They take short, distinctive steps.

Longhair kachina, ***Angak'china***, by Neal David, 14-1/2" h.

Red-bearded **Longhair** kachina, ***Angak'china***, with two kachina heads carved in the base, by Lauren Honyouti, 16" h.

Longhair kachina, ***Angak'china***, by Pochoenix, 6-1/4" h.

47

Longhair kachina, *Angak'china*, with black beard, by Arvin Saufkie, Hopi, 12-1/2" h.

Longhair kachina, *Angak'china*, by Ronald Witt, Hopi, 13" h.

Double-headed Longhair kachina, *Angak'china*, by Brian Kayquaptewa, 20-3/4" h.

Longhair kachina, *Angak'china*, by L. Grover, Jr., 7-1/2" h.

49

Navajo kachina, *Tasap*, by L. Honyouti and Brian Honyouti, 14-3/4" h. Borrowed from and representing the Navajo people, this kachina appears in a line at Plaza Dances. On Third Mesa the name ends with a "p," on Second Mesa with an "f."

Navajo Rain God kachina, ***Tunei-Nili***, by Neil David, 11-1/2" h. This Kachina was inspired by Navajo rain gods who appear on the sixth day of the Navajoo Yeibichai Ceremony. He looks after the Navajo Tasap Kachinas, and sometimes appears with the Velvet Shirt kachinas..

Navajo Blue Masked Yei kachina, *Yei-Bi-Chai*, by L. Jacquez, 9" h.

Navajo Yei kachina, *Yei-Bi-Chai*, in dance position with a drum, 9-1/4" h.

Black Oger kachina, **Nataska**, with bloody saw, by Tino Youvella, 11-1/2" h.

Black Oger, *Nataska*, by Skip Jackson, Polacca, 11-1/2" h. The enforcer, who is a companion of the Ogre Woman, *Soyok Wuhti*, always comes in a pair at the Bean Dance, Powamu Ceremony, in February, wears dark clothes and a wide belt stained red, carries a saw, and makes horrible noises. They are capable of eating children whole if their demand for food and meat for the Ogre Woman is not fulfilled. Children dread them from early life.

Black Ogre kachina, *Awativi Soyok Taka,* with a sword and yucca, by L. Honyouti, 14-3/4" h. He is another companion of the Soyok Wuhti known by the simple breach cloth and spots on his forearms and calves.

Black Ogre kachina, *Awativi Soyok Taka*, by Tino Youvella, 14-1/4" h.

Old Man kachina, *Wuwuyomo*, by Preston Youvella, First Mesa, 8-3/4" h. These old men appear in groups of four in the Bean Dance, Powamu Ceremony, on Third Mesa, where they lead unmarried women into the village. Along the route, they sing songs to encourage the growth of crops for the coming season.

Pot Carrier Man or **Hand** kachina, *Sivu-I-kil taka*, by A. Naha, 10-1/2" h. This Kachina has many names and carries a pot slung on his back by a strap across his chest during Mixed Dances. His legs are generally painted or covered with white pants rather than the customary knitted stockings reserved for chiefs. His neck ruff is cloth.

Pot Carrier Man or **Hand** kachina, *Sivu-i-kil taka*, by Preston Youvella, 7" h.

Priest Killer kachina, *Yo-we*, by Preston Youvella, 6-1/2" h. The legend of the priest killer goes back to the 1600s when pueblo tribes revolted against their Spanish conquerors. The Hopi revolted, too, but were never reconquered. Yo-we was the Kachina that killed a priest at Oraibi. He is shown with the trophy head or a Christian cross symbolic of the priest. He appears only at the Bean Dance, Powamu Ceremony, in February.

Priest Killer kachina, *Yo-we*, by Alexander R. Youvella, First Mesa, 9-1/4" h.

Priest Killer kachina, *Yo-we*, by Nhayah, 12-1/2" h.

Priest Killer kachina, *Yo-we*, by *Kocha Hon Mana*, Jocelyn Honani-Vote, Hopi, 8" h.

Priest Killer kachina, *Yo-we*, by Brian Hanyouti,
14" h.

Priest Killer kachina, *Yo-we*, by Alicia Youvella, First Mesa,
8" h.

Twin War God kachina, by Brendan Kayquoptewa, 15-3/4"
h. He is marked similarly to the Black Ogre, *Awativi Soyok
Taka*, who comes in pairs.

Two Horn kachina, *Alosaka,* by Leo Lacapa, 13" h. *Alsoaka*
is one of the Germ Gods who controls growth and reproduction in all things and is a Sun kachina. He is the Solstice
or Return Kachina for First and Second Mesas. He visits
each kiva, opening it for the return of the Kachinas.

Velvet Shirt kachina, *Navan*, by Brendan Kayquoptewa, 12" h. This Kachina seems to have originated after 1900 in Moenkopi. He is identified with bright colors and flowers and appears in Kiva Dances, *Pamuya* Ceremonies, in January.

61

Velvet Shirt kachina, *Navan*, by Brendan Kayquoptewa,
15-3/4" h.

Velvet Shirt kachina, *Navan*, with a Black-eyed Susan
flower on the base, by Burt Poley, 14" h.

White Chin kachina, *Tuma-uyi*, by L. Honyouti, 10" h. This very old Kachina is not often performed. He comes in a group in the Bean Dance, Powamu Ceremony. His name derives from the white clay used to coat the cottonwood carvings before the kachina dolls are painted.

Witch kachina, *Hilili*, in a dance position, by Lauren Honyouti, 15-1/2" h. Derived from Acoma or Laguna tribes before 1900, this kachina is named for the sound of the shout he makes. He arrived at First Mesa, but the other two mesas disapproved, calling him a witch, or *Powak* Kachina. He evolved as a guard kachina known for rapid dance steps. Now he appears frequently in many dance ceremonies.

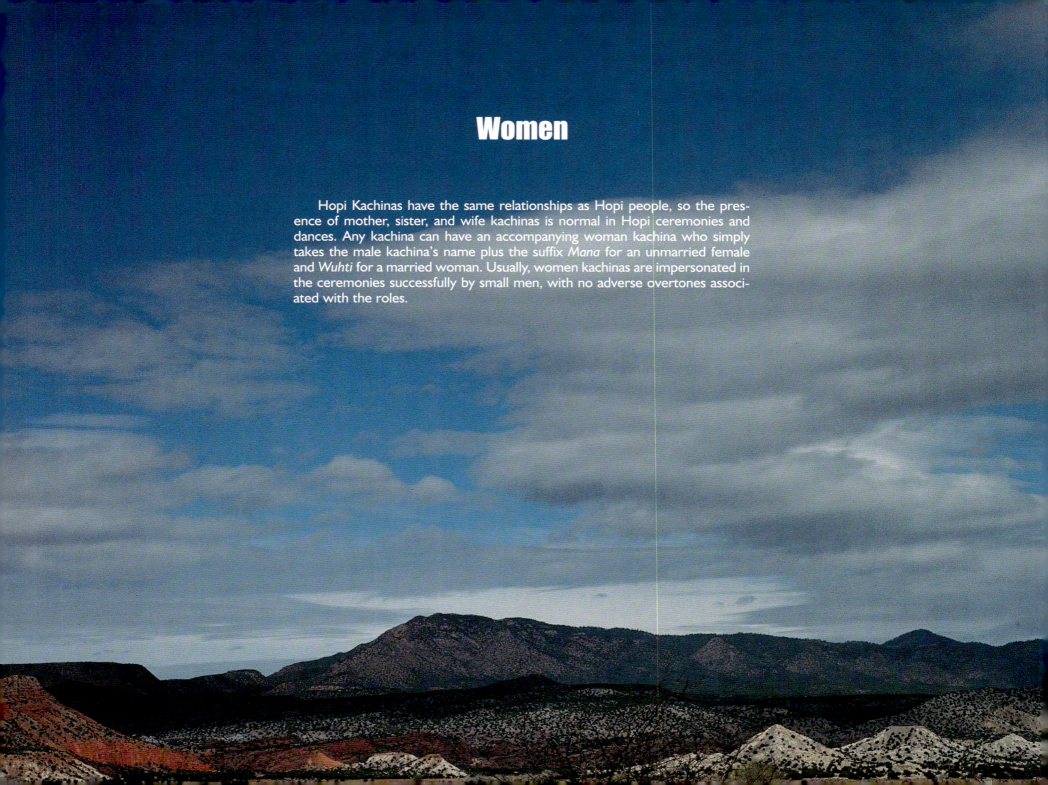

Women

Hopi Kachinas have the same relationships as Hopi people, so the presence of mother, sister, and wife kachinas is normal in Hopi ceremonies and dances. Any kachina can have an accompanying woman kachina who simply takes the male kachina's name plus the suffix *Mana* for an unmarried female and *Wuhti* for a married woman. Usually, women kachinas are impersonated in the ceremonies successfully by small men, with no adverse overtones associated with the roles.

Buffalo Maiden kachina, *Mucias Mana*, by Leo Lacapa, 10" h.

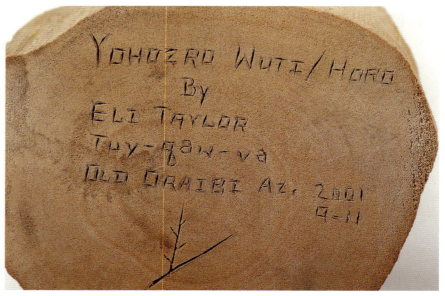

Cold Bringing Woman or **Comb Hair Upwards Girl**
kachina, *Yohozro Wuti* or *Horo Mana*, by Eli Taylor, *Tuy-qaw-va*, of Old Oraibi, 12" h. This is a Tewa kachina that appears during the Bean Dance, or Powamu Ceremony, on First Mesa, in February. She brings cold weather to the Hopi and symbolically carries a hairbrush with her, with which she musses up the hair of people in the audience, like the cold winter wind will do.

Cold Bringing Woman kachina, *Horo Mana*, by Eugene Dawas, 10" h.

Cold Bringing Woman kachina, *Horo Mana*, by Timothy Talawepi, 9-1/2 " h.

Dress kachina, *Kwasai taka*, by Lauren Honyouti, 13" h. This unusual Third Mesa kachina is derived from the Zuni and is named because he wears a dress. His nose is made of three cornhusk packets and lines around his face represent rainbow colors. He carries a bag of corn and a digging stick in his left hand and influences the growth of corn.

Tewa Girl kachina, **_Hano Mana_**, by Jonathan Day, 11-1/2" h. This kachina appears in the Bean Dance, *Powamu* Ceremony, on First Mesa, in February. Her carving likeness is often given to infant and young Tewa girls.

Tewa Girl kachina, **_Hano Mana_**, by Stetson Honymptewa, 14-1/2" h.

Heoto Woman kachina, **Heoto Mana**, in a dance position, by Timothy Talawepi, 5-1/4" h. This woman kachina accompanies the Guard kachina, Heoto, during the Bean Dance parade and at Kiva and Plaza Dances.

70

Kachina Mother or **Pour Water Woman**, *Hahai-i Wuhti*, by Lowell Talashoma, Sr. This kachina has the duty to be mother of all kachinas and dogs, like the Crow Mother. Her real children are monsters like the Nataskas. She appears in important ceremonies with unusual vocal roles. Doll carvers often carve flat versions of Hahai-i Wuhti for infant girls, and later a relief version to them as they grow older. The symbolism is obvious.

Hopi Maidens carving, with dragonflies, by R. Sahmie, 14-3/4" h.

Two **Hopi Maiden** kachinas, by Wally Grover, First Mesa, 11-1/2" h. One has her hair fashioned in two side rolls, a typical Hopi hairstyle version of squash blossoms. The other is a young Crow Mother.

Hopi Maiden with watermelon and prayer bowl, by L. Grover, Jr. 10" h.

Navajo Yei Maiden, by Lee Norcross, 13" h.

Double carving of two **Navajo Yei** kachinas with tablitas, by Corwin Phillips, 22-1/2" h.

Ogre Woman kachina, *Soyok Wuhti*, by Lester Quanimptewa, 9-1/4" h. This monster woman, dressed in black, threatens children with her crook and the knife she carries. She terrifies people with a hideous sound that gave her her name, and bears a basket on her back to carry misbehaving children away.

Ogre Woman kachina, **Soyok Wuhti**, carrying a crook and a knife, with one child mudhead in a backpack and one pulling at her skirt, by Lean Monongye, 12" h.

Ogre Woman kachina, *Soyok Wuhti*, 15" h.

Ogre Woman kachina, *Soyok Wuhti*,
by V. Mahkee, 13-1/2" h.

Ogre Woman kachina, *Soyok Wuhti*,
by Preston Ami, 8-1/4" h.

Snow Maiden kachina, ***Nuvak'china Mana***, by Lowell Talashoma, Sr., 7" h. The Snow Maiden is the counterpart to the Snow Kachina, who brings cold and snow to the Hopis, essential moisture for the crops. She appears primarily at the Niman ceremony praying for cold weather and snow to replenish the ground with moisture.

Snow Maiden kachina, ***Nuvak'china Mana***, by A. Naha, 10-1/2" h.

Snow Maiden kachina, *Nuvak'china Mana*, by
Horace Kayquoptewa, 9-3/4" h.

Snow Maiden, *Nuvak'china Mana*,
by Avohne Naha, 11" h.

The Second Mesa story relates that a young man changed clothing with his bride and was wrapping his hair up like hers when the enemy approached. At Oraibi, a young woman took up her father's weapons to fight the enemy. The kachina is a fierce opponent. During Initiation ceremonies she leads a band of warrior kachinas to protect the procession.

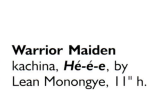

Warrior Maiden kachina, ***Hé-é-e***, by Lean Monongye, 11" h.

Warrior Maiden kachina, ***Hé-é-e*** or ***He Wuhti***, in a dancing position, by Neil David, 7" h. This warrior spirit kachina can be a man in woman's clothing or a woman using a man's equipment, depending on the mesa.

Warrior Maiden kachina, *Hé-é-e*,
by Brendan Kayquoptewa,
13-3/4" h.

82

Warrior Maiden, *Hé-é-e*, kachina, by Tino
Youvella, First Mesa, 9" h.

Warrior Maiden kachina, *Hé-é-e*, by Avohne Naha, 9" h.

Warrior Maiden kachina, *He'e'e*,
by Preston Youvella, 7-1/2" h.

Warrior Maiden kachina, *Hé-é-e*,
by Preston Ami, Hopi Tewa, 9" h.

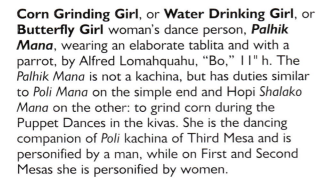

Corn Grinding Girl, or **Water Drinking Girl**, or **Butterfly Girl** woman's dance person, *Palhik Mana*, wearing an elaborate tablita and with a parrot, by Alfred Lomahquahu, "Bo," 11" h. The *Palhik Mana* is not a kachina, but has duties similar to *Poli Mana* on the simple end and Hopi *Shalako Mana* on the other: to grind corn during the Puppet Dances in the kivas. She is the dancing companion of *Poli* kachina of Third Mesa and is personified by a man, while on First and Second Mesas she is personified by women.

Corn-Grinding Girl, *Palhik Mana*, by Jeff James, 17-1/2" h.

Two-doll set, **Corn-Grinding Girl**, *Palhik Mana,* woman with a tablita, and a flat **Crib Toy**, by L. Poola, 20-1/2" h.

Corn-Grinding Girl, *Palhik Mana*, with a tablita, by Merrill Sequi, 12" h.

Corn-Grinding Girl, *Palhik Mana*, by Wayne Poleahla, 17-3/4" h.

Corn-Grinding Girl, *Pahlik Mana*, by Wally Navasie, 9-1/2" h.

Animals

Antelope kachina, *Chof,* by Keith Torres, 13" h. This kachina dances to increase antelope for the hunters. He appears in Kiva Dances and Plaza Dances

Badger kachina of the old style, **Honan**, by Lean Monongye, 10-1/2" h. This old kachina is a healing spirit who receives prayers for growing healing herbs.

Badger kachina of the new style, **Honan**, by Ray Tungovia, 10" h.

Badger kachina, *Honan*, by Tino Youvella, 9" h.

Badger kachina, *Honan*, 11-1/4" h.

Black Bear kachina, *Hon*, by Derrick Hayah, Hopi, 10" h. Bear has the strength to cure the sick. He dances at the winter solstice, Soyala Ceremony, in December at First Mesa. He can appear in different colors.

Bear kachina, *Hon*, by Preston Ami, 9-1/2" h.

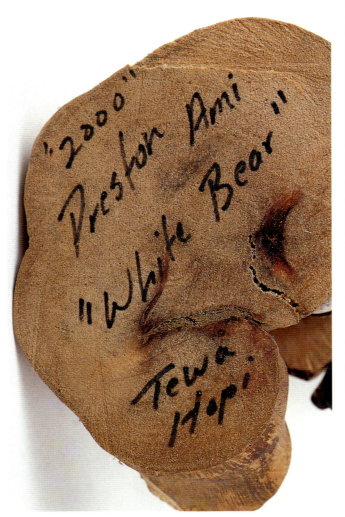

White Bear kachina, **_Kö cha Honau_**, by
Preston Ami, Tewa Hopi, 10-1/4" h.

White Bear kachina, *Köcha Honau*, by Wayne
Poleahla, Old Oraibi, 6" h.

Blue Bear kachina, *Sakwa Honau*,
by R. Sahmie, Hopi, 11-1/2" h.

Bobcat kachina, *Tokoch*, shown kneeling, by Brian Honyouti, 11" h. This kachina appears when work is to be done in the community, only rarely at dances. He looks for people who shirk their responsibilities and tries to prevent idle work.

Buffalo kachina, *Mosairu*, by Leo Lacapa, 10-1/4" h. The Buffalo kachina is always masked, while the Buffalo Dancer is not masked. Otherwise, they look very much alike. The dance is performed to appeal for the increased abundance of buffalo to hunt. He holds a lightning stick and a rattle.

White Buffalo kachina, *Mosairu*, by Preston Youvella, 10-3/4" h.

White Buffalo Dancer, *Mosairu*, by Earl Yowytewa, 9-1/2" h.

White Buffalo Dancer, *Mosairu*, by A. L. Sahmie, Hopi Tewa, 14-1/2" h.

White Buffalo Dancer, *Mosairu*, by Lowell Talashoma, 15" h. The BUffalo dances are usually held in the kivas soon after the kachinas return in the winter. The dance does not include women or female impersonators, as the Social Dance does.

White Buffalo Dancer, *Mosairu*, with leather skirt, yarn tassels, fur mantle and ankle covers, by A. L. Sahmie, Hopi Tewa, 12-1/2" h.

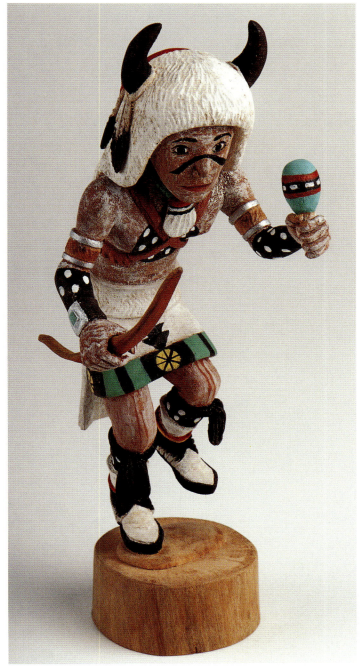

Black Buffalo Dancer, *Mosairu*, with leather skirt, fur head piece, and cloth tassels, by A.L. Sahmie, Hopi Tewa, 14-3/4" h.

White Buffalo Social Dancer, *Mosairu*, by Lowell Talshoma, Sr., 9" h.

Deer kachina, *Sowi-ing*, shown dancing, by Cecil Calnimptewa, 16-3/4" h. The deer has power over rain, so his dance is a prayer for the increase of deer to bring the rain. He is a popular kachina at Plaza Dances, and often is accompanied by the Wolf or Mountain Lion Kachinas.

Deer kachina, *Sowi-ing*, by
William Koots, 14-1/2" h.

Deer kachina, *Sowi-ing*, by L. Grover, Jr. 12" h.

Deer kachina, *Sowi-ing*, by Brian Kayquoptewa, 11-1/4" h.

102

Mountain Lion kachina, *Toho*, by Tino Youvella, 8-1/2" h.
This Kachina appears in the front of grazing animal
kachinas, such as Deer or Antelope, as a side dancer,
because Mountain Lion never gets caught.

Mountain Lion kachina, *Toho*,
by Lowell Talashoma, 12" h.

Mountain Lion kachina, *Toho*, by Brian Honyouti, 8" h.

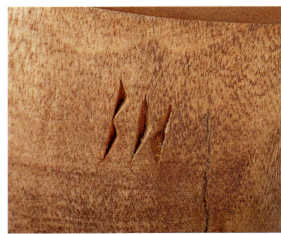

104

Ram kachina, *Pang*, by Tsinnie, 14-1/2" h.

Wolf kachina, *Kweo*, by Keith Torrez, 10-1/2" h. This is a side-dancing kachina with Deer or Antelope, as he represents the bushes he hides behind while watching them. He is naturally a hunter of antelope, so their counterpart kachinas are wary in his presence. He is given cornmeal and prayer feathers after the dances so that he uses his knowledge to capture the game animals.

Wolf kachina, *Kweo*, by Franklin Sahmea, 12" h.

Wolf kachina, *Kweo*,
by Tino Youvella, First Mesa, 9" h.

Wolf kachina, *Kweo*,
by G. Hayah, 14" h.

Wolf kachina, *Kweo*, with a bow, by Lomahquahtu, 17-3/4" h.

Brightly painted **Wolf** kachina, *Kweo*,
Hyeuma, 12-1/2" h.

Wolf kachina, *Kweo*, by W. Grover, 12-1/2" h.

Wolf kachina, *Kweo*, by Brian Kayqueptewa, 13" h.

Fox kachina, *Letaiyo*, and **Crow Mother** kachina, *Angwushnasomitaka*, by Wally Grover, First Mesa, 8-3/4" h. Fox kachina usually appears as a runner and in the winter solstice, Soyala Ceremony, because he is quick.

Birds

Crow Man kachina, *Angwusi*, with a watermelon and **Crow Mother** kachina, *Angwushnasomitaka*, emerging from a kiva, by Alton Pashano, 9-1/2" h. Crow Man Kachina is a warrior that threatens the clowns during Plaza Dances for their absurd behavior

Crow Man kachina, *Angwusi*, with cape and holding yucca, by Avohne Naha, 12" h.

Crow Man kachina, *Angwusi*, in a dancing position, by Henry Naha, 10" h.

Crow Man kachina, *Angwusi*, by Eli Taylor, Old Oraibi, 15-1/4" h.

Crow Bride kachina, *Angwushanai-i*, by L. Honyouti, 14" h. This woman kachina intiates children and talks to the whippers. She carries a tray of corn sprouts and sings softly as she progresses slowly, distributing the corn sprouts, toward the kiva chief. From him she receives prayer feathers and cornmeal before being dismissed. She then moves slowly away, toward her home in the San Francisco Peaks.

Crow Bride kachina, *Angwushanai-i*, by Horace
Kayquaptewa, 10-1/2" h.

Crow Bride kachina, *Angwushanai-i*, by Horace
Kayquaptewa, 10" h.

Crow Bride kachina, *Angushahai-i*, by Eric Kayquoptewa, 10-1/4" h.

Crow Bride kachina, *Angushahai-i*, by Alvin James "Makya," Old Oraibi, 1984, 19-1/2" h.

117

Crow Mother kachina, **Angwushnasomitaka**, shown carrying a bundle of yucca, by Jon Cordero, 13-3/4" h. This dignified and popular kachina nurtures children and furnishes the yucca for their initiation ceremonies.

Crow Mother kachina, *Angwushnasomitaka*, in a dancing position, by Horace Kayquoptewa, 15-1/2" h.

Crow Mother kachina,
Angwushnasomitaka, by
Ronald Honyouti, 10-1/4" h.

120

Crow Mother kachina, *Angwushnasomitaka*, by Lean Monongye, 11" h.

Crow Mother kachina, *Angwushnasomitaka*, 11" h., mounted on a flat board painted with a landscape, by Rod Philips, 21-1/2" h.

Crow Mother kachina, *Angwushnasomitaka*, by
Preton Ami, Tewa Hopi, 11-1/4" h.

Crow Mother kachina, *Angwushnasomitaka*, by
PrestonYouvella, 10-1/2" h.

Miniature **Crow Mother** kachina, *Angwushnasomitaka*, with a kachina emerging from a kiva entrance, by Lawrence Dallas, 2-3/4" h.

Crow Mother kachina, *Angwushnasomitaka*, by Preston Ami, Hopi Tewa, 6-1/4" h. and **Snow Maiden** kachina, **Nuvak'china Mana**, by Horace Kayquoptewa, 11" h.

Crow Mother kachina, *Angwushnasomitaka*, by Nhayah, 13-1/2" h.

Crow Mother kachina, *Angwushnasomitaka*, by R. Kasero, Sr., Hopi, 9-3/4" h.

Crow Mother kachina, *Angwushnasomitaka*, by Arthur Holmes, 13" h.

Eagle kachina, *Kwahu*, and **Mudhead** clown, *Koyemsi*, by Henry Naha.

126

Eagle kachina, **Kwahu**, by Ron Duwyenie, 14-1/2"
h. Eagle dancers are popular because they are
particularly skilled at imitating the movement and
cry of the eagles they personify.

Eagle kachina, **Kwahu**,
by Ron Duwyenie, 8-3/4" h.

Eagle kachina, *Kwahu*, dancing in front of the pueblo, by Leslie David.

Eagle kachina, *Kwahu*, by
Joseph Duwyenie, 9-1/2" h.

Eagle kachina, *Kwahu*, by Coolidge C. Roy, 15" h.

Eagle kachina, *Kwahu*, with an arched rock, by Coolidge Roy, Jr., 10-1/2" h.

Eagle kachina, *Kwahu*, by Coolidge Roy, Jr.,
6-1/2" h.

Eagle kachina, *Kwahu*, by Les David, 10-1/2" h.

Eagle kachina, *Kwahu*, with a corn stalk and clouds, by Les David, 6" h.

Eagle kachina, *Kwahu*, by Les David, 8-1/4" h.

133

Eagle kachina, *Kwahu*, in two tall posts, by Jed Francis, Hopi, 25" h.

Eagle kachina, *Kwahu*, looking down, by Les David, 7-1/2" h.

Eagle kachina, *Kwahu*, during a Night Dance with kiva, pueblo, and three miniature **Mudhead** clowns, by Eric Kayquaptewa, 6-3/4" h.

Eagle kachina, *Kwahu*, by Coolidge Ray, Jr., 14-1/2" h.

Eagle kachina, *Kwahu*, by A. Naha, 14" h.

Eagle kachina, *Kwahu*, dancing out of a pottery bowl, by Lomahquahtu, 22" h.

Eagle kachina, *Kwahu*, by Henry Naha, 10-1/4" h.

Eagle kachina, *Kwahu*, dancing before flowers.

Eagle kachina, *Kwahu*, by *Gai-nah-ne*, Ray Jose, Hopi, 11-1/4" h.

Left-handed Hunter kachina, *Suy-ang-e vif*, and **Great Horned Owl** kachina, *Mongwa*, hanging a killed deer from a tree, by Alfred Lomahquahu, "Bo," 23" h.

Great Horned Owl
kachina, **Mongwa**, by
Brendan Kayquoptewa, 10"
h. This owl Kachina is
constantly at war with the
clowns for their un-respect-
ful behavior. They bring
tension to the ceremonies
and humor to the crowd.

Great Horned Owl
kachina, *Mongwa*, in a
dance position, by
Duane Hyeoma, 12" h.

143

Great Horned Owl kachina, *Mongwa*, by Ray
Tungovia, Polacca, 12-1/4" h.

Great Horned Owl kachina, *Mongwa*, by Tino
Youvella, First Mesa, 10-1/2" h.

Screech Owl kachina, *Hotsko*, by Derrick Hayah, 10-1/2" h. The Screech Owl Kachina appears at Kiva Dances on First Mesa as a predator to small and domestic birds.

Double carving of two kachinas, **Great Horned Owl, *Mongwa***, and **Left-handed Hunter**, ***Suy-ang-e vif***, hanging a killed deer, by Lomahquahtu, 17-1/2" h.

Parrot kachina, *Kyash*, in a dancing position, by Brendan Kayquoptewa, 5-1/4" h. This is new kachina doll since 1965, when it a Parrot Dance was introduced. The Kachina is responsible for summer growth and the increase of colorful parrots, whose feathers are appreciated.

Parrot kachina, *Kyash*, by Eric Kayqueptewa, 9" h.

Butterfly Girl, **Palhik Mana**, with a parrot, shown as a woman seated on rocks, by Alfred Lomahquahtu, 17" h.

Quail kachina, *Kakashka*, painting a crib toy, by Sheldon Talas, Polacca, 7-1/2" h.

Red-Tail Hawk kachina, *Palakwayo*, by Joseph Duwyenie, 10" h. Palakwayo is a chief kachina on Second Mesa and is important on Third Mesa during the Bean Dance, *Powamu* Ceremony.

Rooster kachina, *Kowaku*,
by Ronald Honyumptewa, 8-1/2" h.

Snipe kachina, **Patszro**, with arms/wings raised, by Fred Chapella, 9-3/4" h. this Kachina appears in Kiva Dances connected with the Bean Dance, Powamu Ceremony. He is responsible for the increase in snipes for hunters.

Snipe kachina, **Patszro**, with butterfly carving on front of the base, by Nhayah, 13" h.

Plants

Home Dance kachina,
Niman, by Leo Lacapa, 16" h.
Niman kachina sometimes
substitutes for *Hemis* kachina
in the Home Dance. This is the
ceremony of the first crop's
harvest and completing the
kachina season.

153

Zuni Ripened Corn kachina, *Sio Hemis*, with a large tablita, by Leo Lacapa, 14-1/2" h.

Zuni Ripened Corn kachina, *Sio Hemis*, with a large tablita, by Ferrel Susunkewa, 12" h.

154

Qöqöle kachina kneeling, by Jon Cordero, 7-1/2" h. This kachina appears only at Third Mesa during the Winter Solstice, Soyala Ceremony, to open the kivas. But he also can be seen squatting on the ground shooting marbles. He wears old-style Anglo clothing and wears a black mask with blue markings.

155

Flower kachina, *Tsitoto,* carrying a pine tree, by Lean Monongye, 10-1/2 " h. This kachina dances in many ceremonies, especially the Bean Dance, Powamu Ceremony, in February. He wears a mask with rainbow stripes and carries a pine tree.

Broadleaf Yucca Old Man kachina, *Samo-a-Wutaka*, by Stetson Honyumptewa, 9-1/4" h. This Kachina appears in the Bean Dance at Hano, representing the spirit of the sweet cactus fruit, such as agave and yucca. He knows many songs that will bring clouds to water the crops. He appears with clowns at Mixed Dances in the spring, usually wearing old and shabby clothing.

Squash kachina, *Patung*, by Tino Youvella, First Mesa, 9" h. The Squash Kachina appears on First Mesa as a runner. Usually he carries the squash flower in his right hand and yucca in his left hand. To him prayers for healthy crops are made.

Squash kachina, *Patung*, by Lean Monongye,
7-1/2" h.

160

Green Squash kachina, *Patung*, playing a flute, by Lowell Taloshoma, Sr., 14-1/2" h.

Squash adult and child kachina set, *Patung*, by Keith Torrez, 11" h.

Insects and Reptiles

Butterfly kachina, *Poli k'china*, by Neal Naha, 16-1/2" h. This kachina appears with his female counterpart, *Poli Mana*, in the kiva for the Night Dance on Third Mesa.

Butterfly Maid kachina, **Poli Mana**, with tablita, by Jeff James Nuvahongnaya, 13' h.

Dragonfly kachina, *Sivuftotovi*, in an interpretation that looks like red corn, by Eugene Hamilton, Deer Foot, 9" h. Dragonfly is a runner that carries corn smut he smears on people.

Frog kachina, *Paqua*, by Lowell Talashoma, 6-1/2" h.

Hornet kachina, *Tatangya*, shown painting a crib toy, by Sheldon Talas, Polacca, 6-1/2" h.

Racer Snake kachina, *Lölökong,* by Leo Lacapa, 13" h.

Robber fly kachina, *Kokopelli*, by Nhayah, 12-3/4" h. To the Hopi, this popular kachina plays a flute only when he borrows the instrument to dance. He appears in the Mixed Kachina Dances and Night Dance. He is credited with bringing babies and hunting.

Robber fly kachina, *Kokopelli*, by Derrick Hayah, 10-1/2" h.

Snake on skirt kachina, *Situlili*, by Leo Lacapa, 12-1/2" h. Common on Second Mesa, this kachina acts as a guard in the Powamu Ceremony.

169

Sand Snake kachina, *Tuwa-tcua*, by Roger Suehopka, 12-3/4" h.

Yellow Sand Snake kachina, *Sikya Tuwa-tcua*, by Collateta, 15" h.

Clowns

Clowns are not Kachinas, but important comic actors who influence Hopi ceremonies. Today, clowns are popular carvings made by kachina doll carvers, and many fine and extensive collections of Hopi clown carvings have been formed. Each area of Hopiland has its own clown style, the Bahnimptewa and Wright book identifies seven types: Koyemsi or Mudhead, Koyala or Koshari, Piptuka, Pipu Wuhti, Tsuku, Kaisale, and White Cloud. They appear at most Plaza Dances and in may of the major ceremonies. Many times they illustrate improper behavior and demonstrate outrageous humor, but also may provide necessary functions in the ceremonies.

Two **Hopi Tewa Clowns**, by Nhayah, 7-1/2" h.

Second Mesa Clown with watermelon in an action position, by Lowell Talashoma, Sr. 16-1/2" h.

"**Happy New Year**" carving of a seated clown with basketball, train on a round track, and yellow pick-up toy, by Alfred Lomahquaku, 4-3/4" h.

Basketball Player clown over a Christmas tree, by Alfred Lomahquaku, 4" h.

Hano Clown eating a hamburger,
by Neil David, 9" h.

Hano Clown with two watermelons, by Neil
David, 6-1/2" h.

Hano Clown with a log and hatchet, by Preston Youvella, 14" h.

Hano Clown shown catching a chicken, by Neil David 8-1/2" h.

Two **Hano Clown**s, by Neil
David, 6" h. and 7-1/2" h.

Hano Clown, by Leroy Jim, Hopi, 11" h.

Hano Clown holding a dog, by
Neil David, 9-1/2" h.

Ho-e Clown in the Bean Dance, with a drum, by Brian
Honyouti 11" h.

Koyala Clown, by Felix Harvey, 14-1/2" h.

Koshari Clown eating watermelon and quite animated, by Lowell Talashoma, 15-1/4" h.

Koshari Clown, by Neil David, 5-1/4" h.

Above and Below:
Three Koshari Clowns, set depicting See-, Speak-, & Hear-No-Evil, by John David, 6-1/2" h.

Koshari Clown seated and eating watermelon, with leather bag, skirt and tassels, by Clarence Cleveland, 13-1/2" h.

Koshari Clown, by Silas Roy, 9-3/4" h.

Koshari Clown and **Great Horned Owl** kachina, *Mongwa*,
by Keith Torrez, 10" h.

Mocker clown, *Kwikwilyaka*, shown at a campfire with an axe, one foot in a moccasin and one in a sneaker shoe, by Jon Cordero, 6" h.

Mudhead Clown, *Koyemsi*, carrying **Paralyzed** kachina, *Tuhavi*, 12-1/2" h.

Double **Mudhead Clown**, *Koyemsi*, by Brian Honyouti, 10-1/2" h.

Mudhead Clown, *Koyemsi,* by Lowell Talashoma, 6-1/4" h.

Warrior Mudhead Clown, *Koyemsi,* by Orin Poley, 14" h.

Mouse, by Finkle Sahmie, Polacca, 8-1/4" h. This figure is not a clown or a kachina, but a Second Mesa legend. Mouse decided to get rid of the bothersome chicken hawk. He bated the hawk and lured him to dive toward a kiva and impale himself on the ladder pole, thus ending the legend. Often he is known as Warrior Mouse, out of respect for his deed.

Warrior Mouse, by Joseph M. Torivio, Second Mesa, 11-3/4" h.

References

Bromberg, Erik. *The Hopi Approach to the Art of Kachina Doll Carving*, Atglen, Pennsylvania: Schiffer Publishing Ltd., 1986.

Day, Jonathan S., *Traditional Hopi Kachinas, A New Generation of Carvers*, Flagstaff: Northland Publishing, 2000.

Wright, Barton. *Hopi Kachinas, The Complete Guide to Collecting Kachina Dolls*. Flagstaff: Northland Publishing, 2000.

_____. Kachinas, *A Hopi Artist's Documentary*. Original paintings by Cliff Bahnimptewa. Flagstaff: Northland Press with the Heard Museum, Phoenix, 1985.

Glossary

Awta- a bow and arrow

Aya- a rattle

Banana- a white man

Dremel- an electrically-powered tool used to carve some of the contemporaty dolls

Hahay'iwuuti- the first crib toy doll given to a child

Hano- the eastern third of First Mesa where the Tewa live

Honngaapi- bear root

Kachin tihu- a Hopi kachina doll

Kachin Tithu- plural of kachin tihu

Kachina- a spirit in the Hopi world that is represented at ceremonies by a human

Kiva- the underground ceremonial chamber for religious activities

Mana- an unmarried female of marriageable age

Moqui- an early term for Hopi

Paho- a cottonwood prayer stick or prayer feathers, thought to be the antecedent of the kachina doll

Pahaana- a name for non-Indian (Anglo) people and a legendary, lost white Hopi brother

Piki- A wafer-thin flat bread served during Hopi ceremonies

Puchtiku- a flat crib-toy doll

Shalako- A kachina ceremony rarely conducted, perhaps once in a decade, during Niman, and some of the specialized the kachinas that take part in it.

Sakwatootsi- Blue Hopi moccasins

Sumiviki- a Hopi sweet food

Tablita- the flat, upright, wooden headpiece of a female dancer, often highly decorated

Taka- a man

Tewa- people who emigrated from the Rio Grande, around the year 1700, to First Mesa

Tovokimpi- a bullroarer, piece of cottonwood root tied to a string and swung hard in a circular motion during ceremonies to create a deep sound like wind and help bring the rain

Tuma- a paint composed of white clay and pigment

Tusayan- an early Spanish name for Hopiland

Wuhti- a married woman

Wu'ya- the ancestral spirit of a clan

Index